DAW
OF THE NEW AGE

5

**New Agers relate
their search for the truth**

PENFOLD BOOKS

Contents

Chapter	Title	Author	Pg.
Introduction			3
1.	Out of the Twilight Zone	Paul James-Griffiths	4
2.	Sai Baba: Lord of the Air	Tal Brooke	11
3.	From Chaos to Cosmos	Alan Morrison	22
4.	Inside The New Age Nightmare	Randall Baer	31
5.	Outer Beauty, Inner Despair	Caryl Matrisciana	39
6.	To the Reader		47

Introduction

The New Age is the fastest growing spiritual movement in the West.

New Age philosophy, a complex mixture of Hinduism, Buddhism, Christianity, the occult and humanism, is attracting millions of people who are shopping in the world's spiritual market place for what suits them best.

The following five true-life stories come from New Agers who were determined to discover the ultimate truth they were sure existed 'somewhere' in the maze of writings and experiences available to them.

Each story is unique and will strike a chord with readers who have had any experience of the multi-faceted New Age Movement.

Out of the Twilight Zone

by
Paul James-Griffiths
Enfield, London, England.

Born in Malaysia in May 1962 into a Christian home, I lived for a short time on Penang Island, where my father was serving in the Royal Air Force. After returning to England and reaching my teenage years, I rejected the church as a hypocritical, weak-willed fossil - about as much use as paying real life bills with 'Monopoly' money. I always believed there was something 'out there' and more to life than just what I could 'see', but my experiences in church were enough to put anybody off.

It started at a Roman Catholic convent school. The nuns there, with one or two exceptions, were cruel and apparently unloving. They used to whip us with metal rulers if we ever touched the statues of the saints. A school rumour that God was a fire-breathing half-man, half bull creature who punished small children didn't help! We were ruled by fear. My second experience was at a private boarding school where church services were in Latin and we were beaten if we could not remember the correct responses. When a former monk came to teach us French, we expected him to be a man of God. Instead he sexually abused the boys in the dormitories, until he was caught in the act and thrown out. Thirdly, at a well known English public school, I refused to go to chapel and told the authorities that since God never turned up in church, why should I bother going? To me, there was more life in the graveyard than in church. As a punishment I was forced to run round a running track for

4

three hours before breakfast! I stubbornly dug my heels in and refused to go to chapel at all. My punishment increased weekly until I gave in. Outwardly I acquiesced with religion, but inwardly I hated it. This led to me persecuting anybody I thought was a Christian. We drove one boy away from the school. Another we nearly suffocated to death in a trunk. I was convinced that Christianity was an oppressive system for brainwashing and controlling people. This dogmatic, restrictive regime had been responsible for the Crusades, the Spanish Inquisition and other atrocities. I therefore rejected it and chose instead to seek out an alternative spiritual worldview.

Since childhood I had been open to spiritual things and readily devoured books on ghosts and the supernatural. *Hammer House of Horror* films were my favourite TV programmes. It was not surprising that I began to experiment with ouija boards and astral travel. The deeper I became involved, the more I experienced 'spiritual presences' with me. One day, under the influence of a spirit, I tore down the emergency fire instructions from the back of a dormitory door and wrote down an alternative Ten Commandments. Then, following the directions of this spirit, I formed a cult called the 'Crystal Phlagrammists'. I recruited other rebellious teenagers like myself who were sick of chapel and we began meeting together, first as a laugh, then more seriously. One boy brought in a crystal prism and we began to use it as a focal point of spiritual energy in the room. We would chant, call up the spirit beings of the ancient Egyptian pyramids and practice meditation under red lights, listening to music by Brian Eno and Jean Michel Jarre. It was bizarre. We were reported and I was called in by the housemaster and ordered to stop. The cult disbanded but I continued to fervently pursue the spirit world alone. Sometimes I would visit the old pagan temples in the school grounds, which were devoted to such gods and goddesses as Bacchus, Venus and Diana. In one semi-burnt out building, I used to sit in an occult circle surrounded by magic symbols and call up spirits. I would have visions and encounters with spirit beings. I read Nostradamus, Wordsworth, Shelley and Keats, and I nicknamed my most frequent spirit guide 'The Muse' because of his inspiration and revelations. Two other spirit guides were called 'Brenwyn' and 'Bardon'. I believed these entities were there to assist me on my path of spiritual enlightenment.

5

The Muse began to show me the true spiritual path. God did exist but he was the energy found in all things. To know him we had to release the spiritual potential within us through meditation. This 'cosmic consciousness' was especially strong in religious people who followed intuition rather than reasoning. Materialism and fundamentalist religions had only produced war, greed, inequality, oppression and pollution of the planet. Cultures like the North American Indians and Australian Aborigines did not fight nature, but flowed with it and harmonised with it. They were therefore more advanced than the West. We needed to learn from them and work with nature otherwise there would be no future for planet earth.

God, according to the Muse, was in all religions, and it was merely our ignorance that caused us to think any one religion was the only true one. As we harmonised together with the God consciousness in all of us, we would cease to be divided and become one family, thus bringing in a new era of world peace. I didn't know it at the time, but in the 1970s, thousands of philosophies, therapies and groups were being networked together by spiritual forces with the same overall vision, although expressed in a variety of ways. We now know this grouping as the 'New Age Movement'.

At the age of 17 I began to write, under the Muse's guidance, a Tolkien style fantasy novel called 'Mantheus', which he promised would be used to spread this teaching. As I neared the completion of the first draft of the book, an extraordinary thing happened. A strange drowsiness came over me, so I lay down and shut my eyes. I experienced a powerful vision, which was 'virtual reality' and seemed three-dimensional. One minute I was flying very fast over cities of the world; then I was hurtling down a dark tunnel. Before I knew it, I was in an ancient oak panelled corridor. There was a row of open doors on either side of the corridor and my spirit guide was standing in duplicate form outside each door. As I passed the doors he was beckoning me to enter. A force tried to pull me in, but a greater force prevented me. Each room had no back wall, but was a different spiritual dimension. I saw strange and amazing scenes in each room but always the powerful force stopped me from entering. Finally, I was allowed to enter a room on the far left. Inside was a long wooden table at which my spirit guide was sitting, with a huge leather bound book lying open on the table before him.

As soon as I entered, he smiled and beckoned me to come and sign the book, but that strange powerful force lifted me clear out of the room, until I saw the Muse far below. I was brought to a place where I saw a king sitting on a throne, surrounded by angels and people in white robes. I saw the earth on fire below me in another dimension. The king opened a gate and showed me a glorious garden where a crystal river ran between fruit trees, and the presence of love, beauty, peace and joy filled the place. When I finally came back to my senses I was trembling with awe and wonder. I felt that this was God warning me to cease my occult involvement immediately. I contacted a local priest, and despite getting christened and confirmed, I did not come to know God personally.

In 1981 I went to Australia and met some Christian relatives who explained that Jesus Christ was truly God, and that He had died on a cross to pay for all my guilt and sin. They said Christ had risen from the dead and was alive in heaven. They told me I needed to be born again by repenting and believing in the Lord Jesus. However, it was while I was on a survival trip in some rainforests in Cape Tribulation, Queensland, that I read the book of Revelation (the last book in the Bible) and was amazed to find that part of my vision was contained there. I also read the words of Jesus, *"Behold, I stand at the door and knock, if any man hear my voice and open the door, I will come in."* There and then I simply prayed to the Lord Jesus Christ, handing him my guilt and sin and asking him to come into my soul. The sense of peace, acceptance and joy that filled me was indescribable. It felt as if a weight had fallen off my shoulders. I knew I had found the Lord at last, and He had found me.

After being baptised in Alice Springs, I returned to England to commence my University studies. Upon my return, the spirit guides came and tried to strangle me. Their hatred for me, the 'traitor', was strong. But through prayer, the Lord delivered me from their attacks. At Leicester University I received a degree in Classical Studies and World Religions. My two Professors on the course taught that all religions led to God; despite both having been ministers in Christian denominations. Although I was now a true Christian I was confused. I began to study the Bhagavad Gita, the Buddhist Scriptures and the Muslim Qu'ran in depth, as well as some tribal religions and the ancient religions of Babylon, Egypt, Persia, Greece and Rome. While reading the Bhagavad Gita, I discovered that Krishna (an important Hindu god) had said: *"I am the source from which all creatures evolve*" (Bhagavad Gita 0:8). He also said he was the 'door' through whom we had to go to find salvation. He claimed to be the 'Father', the 'goal of life', the 'Lord', the 'one true friend' and the 'inner witness' (B.G. 9:17, 18).

However, I found out from reading the Bible that Jesus stated of Himself: "*I am the Way, the truth and the life, nobody comes to the Father except through me*" (John 14:6). He also claimed to be the 'door' through which we have to enter to be saved (John 10:9). Then one day I came across the Bible verse, "*And if Christ has not been raised, your faith is vain* [worthless], *you are yet in your sins*" (1 Corinthians 15:17). From the context of the verse, I realised that Jesus Christ had physically been raised from the dead. This was not a spiritual reappearance, nor a reincarnation; it was literal and physical resurrection. I realised that no other religious leader in history had ever risen from the dead, thus justifying their claims. If Jesus truly rose, then He was unique and stood supreme.

For months I read the Bible, often from evening until breakfast to 'get at the truth'. I discovered that Jesus had fulfilled hundreds of prophecies written in the Old Testament about the coming life and work of the Messiah. This gripped me with excitement; no other religious leader had such credentials. Finally the day came, at about midnight one evening, when I cried out, "*It is true! Jesus Christ is the only true God and Saviour for mankind. There is none other! He has truly risen from the dead!* " I piled all my religious books such as Nostradamus, the Bhagavad Gita, Qu'ran, Buddhist Scriptures, Von Daniken's 'Chariots of the Gods' at one end of the desk, and my Bible at the other. "*There!*" I said, "*Jesus Christ and the Bible belong here, alone in truth, and you lot belong a million miles away!* " From that time until now, I have been unshakeable in my belief in Christ as the only Saviour. I have proved him by experience in many wonderful ways, and by thorough investigation.

Looking back now, I am amazed to see how Satan deceived me, from one layer of deception to the next. I refer to this as Satan's 'onion principle'. Being aware of my disillusionment with established religion, Satan offered an exciting alternative spirituality to which I easily succumbed. Outwardly, the philosophy of universalism, with its promise of unity and world peace was attractive. The key to holding everything together was pantheism - the belief that God is an energy or force that permeates the whole universe. Through meditation, I was trying to find oneness with God - a feature common to all the Eastern occult based religions. The spirit guides were there to assist me in this process and to use me as a vessel for their message. I would freely quote from the Bible, Hindu, Buddhist and Muslim Scriptures in a dishonest attempt to make all religions merge and so avoid contradictions and possible areas of conflict. The Muse convinced me that the Christians had misrepresented Lucifer. He was not the devil, but Pan the god of nature, who worked through the process of evolution for humanity's benefit. He had a network of many spirits in nature, which wanted to align with human beings to save the earth. I was informed that extremism was the real cause of conflict and disharmony. Orthodox, 'organised' religion was one extreme and Satanism the other. What I needed to do was strike a balanced and thus promote true 'wholeness'.

It was years later that I read some of the most influential books in the New Age Movement by Madame Blavatsky, Alice Bailey and others. I was stunned to find that their spirit guides had propagated the same philosophy as mine. At the heart of the onion is a belief in Lucifer. Blavatsky states openly that Lucifer is the real god of enlightenment and that the Biblical God, Jehovah, is the enemy of Universalism. Indeed, this is the view of Freemasonry, Gnosticism, witchcraft and most leaders in the New Age Movement. I even discovered that the famous *Findhorn Community* was based on the same principles. As I read the Bible with a humble attitude, I began to see how warped I had become, despite my well-meaning intentions. The Bible showed me what I was really like 'inside', compared with how righteous and loving the true God is. I no longer dishonestly discarded the real contradictions I found in other religious books; rather I faced up to their problematic sayings and practices. For example, the Hindu god Krishna says, *"I am Prahlada, born among demons... I am the gambling of the gamblers"* (B.G. 10: 30, 36). I could not accept such a god.

Readers of the 'wisdom' of the *Upanishads* are told to worship the sun daily, to cleanse themselves from sin, and to worship the moon for prosperity (Kausitaki-Brahmana Upanishad, 2:7-8). Digging deeper I found actual black magic, plus an abundance of pure superstition in these sacred writings. I discovered the god Shiva was also called Bhudapati, 'Prince of demons,' a Biblical description for Beelzebub or Satan. Shiva originated the system of yoga with its 'Kundalini' (psychic energy) and system of 'chakras' (energy points apparently in the spiritual body), to try to bring his disciples into union with Brahman - or to realise their godhood, the lie of Satan in the garden of Eden (see Genesis 3:5). Shiva too, in Hindu literature, has a schizophrenic nature. On one hand he is a celibate and an ascetic, on the other hand he is a sex maniac who commits adultery with scores of women when their husbands are away from home. Understandably therefore, many Gurus who follow his path appear to be 'holy' and serene, demonstrating amazing psychic ability, yet are constantly involved in sexual immorality. Being 'God' however, they claim to be above the law!

While I was a 'mystic' seeking utopia through occult philosophy, never did I realise that I was being used as a tool of Satan. Today, as I observe the spiritual scene, I see religious leaders from 'Christian' churches involved in interfaith services (in Cathedrals!) which promote pantheistic philosophy I read about in Satanic literature. This same philosophy is mushrooming everywhere in alternative medicine, music, the media and the education system. Indeed, it is now a global movement preparing the way for the coming Antichrist who will be Satan's 'world President'. No wonder my spirit guides tried to kill me as I tried to break free of their grip. Their true identity was revealed as the mask of peace, love and unity was swept away.

In 1990 I went to hear the New Age leader Benjamin Crème in London. He spoke about the coming Maitreya, who would be the future world leader. Creme said this leader would be recognised as the Christ for the Christians, Messiah for the Jews, Buddha for the Buddhists, Krishna for the Hindus, the Imam Mahdi for the Muslims and a world Saviour for the humanists. This leader would demonstrate phenomenal miraculous power and achieve world peace. Anybody who would not accept him would be 'removed' to another 'dimension'. As I looked around at the mainly professional audience, who appeared to be hanging onto his every word, I recalled how I too had once 'been there', preparing the way for the antichrist in total ignorance. How thankful I am to have found the true God and Saviour, the Lord Jesus Christ who said, *"And you shall know the truth, and the truth shall make you free"* (John 8:32).

Sai Baba: Lord of the Air

by
Tal Brooke
Berkeley, California, USA.

My urge to go to India upon graduating from the University of Virginia was a predictable reaction after years of searching. Maybe it all started when I heard my first ghost story, or got an ouija board at the age of ten. Or perhaps when I was 'into' flying saucers and ESP in my teens, and later LSD. Whatever it was, I knew that I had to settle the issue of truth.

After only three months of wandering across India, I was disillusioned. The land ran amuck with mind-destroyed children, and all the famous gurus had failed the test - J. Krishnamurti, the Ramakrishna Mission, Maharishi Mahesh Yogi, Kirpal Singh and many others. Of the remaining options I chose Sai Baba. Practically every Indian I met swore to his authenticity, claiming that he was Lord Krishna and Christ re-born.

When I met Sai Baba, he worked a miracle. Then he prophesied great things. When I saw the huge crowds around him, his magnetic charisma and his immense powers, I was almost certain that I had finally found a real 'Master' in India, and that his messianic claims were true. I was his closest foreign disciple for almost two years. I wrote a book for him, spoke before vast audiences, and was given endless personal favours by

11

Baba; then the tables suddenly turned on me. The perfect bubble exploded, and I entered the deepest depression of my life, trying to avoid facing up to the inevitable conclusion: Baba, despite his powers, was not divine. He was a false messiah.

What motives could such a metaphysical pied piper have? The answer lay in a book I had looked down my nose at for a long time: the Torah of the prophets and the Gospels of the apostles. But it had taken two extraordinary years in India, and deep explorations into mysticism, to come that far.

I stood in the large, walled compound of a private residence, on the outskirts of the city of Ananthapur in Andhra Pradesh. It was 1970. That particular evening, forty or fifty Indian devotees watched as three limousines entered the driveway. In the back seat of the main car was a figure in a brilliant red gown, his hair raised up Afro-style. This was Bhagavan Sri Sathya Sai Baba, the most powerful spiritual personage in all of India. As he emerged from the car, I felt an instant shock wave it would be hard to describe.

Undoubtedly Baba was the most magnetic being I had ever seen. I felt a second jolt as I saw Baba talking to an Indian who was making some kind of request. But Baba knew already, telling the devotee the problem before he could even get the words out. As the devotee's mouth dropped in awe, Baba pulled up his sleeve. He spun his arm in circles with the open palm down - and suddenly the hand was no longer empty. A miracle! From nowhere he had produced a handful of grey powder that he was now pouring into the devotee's hand, telling him to eat it.

Baba's spontaneous access to people's thoughts could only be explained by a key idea of vedanta, the concept of 'thoughtless-all-knowing'. Only an enlightened person, without the limiting ego, could harbour the infinite impersonal mind of God. Baba, then, was a kind of walking doorway into the absolute. When he talked or acted, it was not simply as a man: he was a meeting-point with the Godhead. I wasn't sure what I was supposed to do. I noticed that a few people came up to Baba, knelt down, and touched his feet. I walked up to Baba. Doing what the Indians call *pada namaskar*, I knelt down and touched my head on Baba's feet, remaining there as he patted my back saying, "*Very happy, very happy.*"

The owner of the house called me aside and said, "*You are indeed very fortunate that Bhagavan has plans for you. Just accept these things by faith. They are no mere coincidences, but the will of God.*"

Our life with Baba soon settled into a pattern. We Western devotees went to the daily morning *darshan* (discourse), heard a few words from Baba, and then went home till the afternoon *darshan*. We relished each word spoken by Baba, and every little intuition, dream or psychic experience that any of us had. Early in May 1971, Baba gave us our tenth interview in two weeks. Somebody asked about *sadhana* (spiritual practices) and Baba replied: "*There are many methods. One is japa. Choose a name of God; whatever name you choose, that is also mine - Rama, Krishna, Shiva, Baba - all of them. Then close the eyes, sit in quiet and repeat with bhakti* [adoration] *calling to God.*

"*Another method is dhyanam, concentration, with or without form. Sit on the floor in the quiet, with your back straight and your legs in padma asana* [full lotus or half lotus]. *Look straight ahead, concentrating on the tip of the nose. Then concentrate on one of the forms of God. After a while you become that form. For meditation without form, use a flame - jyoti is light, symbol of God. Imagine the flame in the middle of the brow. Let this light destroy all hate, anger, ego and jealousy and let it fill the body. Keep the head straight, from the base of the spine up.*"

Baba reached down and positioned me in the meditation posture, which was quite an effort to hold. "*Then when purification comes, the energy, called kundalini shakti, can pass from the base of the spine tip. Then one day, it will pass all the way tip and - bas - enlightenment! The play is over!*"

Enlightenment is no easy matter. Without grace, Baba emphasised, it would be impossible to attain. "*Grace is always coming from God, showering like rain from the clouds. But the devotee must be willing to hold the cup to receive God's grace. Trust the Lord, and have no doubt, sir. Then the tiny holes of doubt can be repaired by steady sadhana, spiritual discipline.*"

In the private moments I had spent with Baba so far, I had made considerable leaps of faith. The week before I had found myself

13

declaring, *"I want to love you with all my heart and soul, Baba. I want your will to be mine. I know you are God."* This time, however, I was far less satisfied about myself. *"What do you want?"* Baba asked. *"Baba, I can't stand the evil in myself. Help me get rid of it; anything that holds me back."* With patient understanding, Baba ran through my sins. *"Too many bad thoughts, impure sanskaras* [trait from past lives]. *Thoughts of material things: anger, jealousy, hate, ego and thoughts of girls. No good."*

Baba wrapped his arms about me and hugged tightly. If the hallmark of this session with him was my own impurity, I thought, then I was under a spiritual microscope as never before. The embrace of Radha-Krishna, the *avatar* of the *Dwarka Yuga* (Baba) and his lover (me) was the highest resolution of two polarities. My inner voice likened the embrace with Baba to the meeting of cosmic lovers. God and God, breaking the wall of *maya* to merge. Baba's hug grew tighter. Then a thought crept out of some dark abyss. His breathing is deeper, more intense. Why does he need to twist his pelvis in this way? Is this some strange divine passion? Am I warping something that is innately pure with the evil of my own suspicions? My mind was reeling. Was the test not only that I comply, but that I see and know the holy in Baba's act? The Indian scriptures declared repeatedly, *"Anything done in total purity is without blemish."* My belief in Baba's deity began to outweigh surface appearances. *"Too much at stake. I have got to believe in him. Lust contradicts Baba's nature; therefore it does not exist in him. He cannot sin, because it is not in him to do so. Blind faith. Baba is innocent. And what about his miracles?"*

The crowds had gathered for the great festival. That night all over India the Saivite sect would be paying homage to the great lord Shiva, god of destruction in the Hindu triune godhead. Those across India who recognised the avatarhood of Sathya Sai Baba would dwell on his name and form, singing *bhajans* to him in family halls. He was considered by the Saivite sect to be Shakti-Shiva the male and female principles of the universe combined. They and the devotees of Vishnu agreed that he was Narayana, God come to earth with human and divine attributes.

All over India, Baba's five million devotees were hoping that tonight Baba's miracles would bring them to *sat-chit-ananda* - the being,

14

consciousness, and bliss of the absolute. Freed from their painful, tragic existence, they would emerge into a state of infinite, ecstatic awareness. Baba chanted a *sloka* from the *Bhagavad Gita,* stretching his arms like a bird: *"Renounce all dharmas: and take refuge in me alone. I will liberate you from all sins; grieve not."*

After forty minutes speaking Baba paused, looked at the audience, and fell back into his seat. He looked away as though concealing great pain. Though his head jerked in spasms, his smiles of reassurance gently told us not to worry. This indestructible man was taking on the infinite torments that we deserved. His grace was covering our debts of *karma.* Suddenly Baba lurched forward. In an explosive movement, a brilliant stone - a sacred *lingam* (phallus) larger than an egg - shot out of his mouth onto a handkerchief. Baba held the object high for everybody to see it shining. Then he set it down on the table in full view, spun round and went out.

"Special grace," Baba announced. I concentrated on his bare forearm whirling around, and felt a surge of energy, as his palm closed. When he opened his hand there were five rings, each neatly plaited from seven strands of metal. The girls sighed as they put them on and studied them; each ring was the perfect fit for its wearer. Baba looked over to the male half of the room. His hand began whirling again in huge arcs. Another surge rippled through the room only this time Baba's hand was holding something so large that it glinted through his fingers. Baba opened his hands to reveal eleven oval metal plates with a photographic likeness of himself enamelled on each of them.

Near the end of this interview, he briefly left the room and returned with a computer card which he handed to a woman called Gill. *"You couldn't have done that"*, Gill exclaimed, *"I just mailed off my claim a few days ago."* Gill had suddenly noticed that the card, from the San Francisco branch of the Bank of America, happened to have that day's date stamped on it. Not even a private Phantom jet could clock up that sort of time. *"I have the whole world in the palm of my hand,"* Baba replied. *"Divine will, sir. Space and time are no obstacle to Swami."*

We followed Baba back to the town of Whitefield with his final words of the birthday festival echoing loudly in our minds; *"I am the embodiment*

15

of truth. This is the first time in history that mankind has had the chance of being with me in this number. The moment you come into my presence, all your sins are forgiven. Do not try to compare my power with those petty powers of magicians. My power is divine and has no limit. I have the power to change the earth into the sky and the sky into the earth. I am beyond any obstacle and there is no force, natural or supernatural, that can stop my mission or me. Do not lose this chance, it is more important than you will ever realise. Do not forfeit the chance to be in my presence." The impression made on us was vivid. Sai Baba was clearly not a human being. A human body he had, but he did not think or operate as other people did.

A few days later Baba gave us the first group interview since we had returned to the town of Puttaparthi. Baba started out on a sweet note; "*You see the dhobis going to the Chitravati river every day, cleaning and beating the clothes on the rocks? Well, I am spiritual dhobi. I am the best dhobi, cleaning the minds of my devotees - every day with love.*"

"*Baba,*" I said, "*Ed* [a friend of mine] *wants to be your disciple. Came all the way to India to see you. Now he wants your permission and a letter to stay.*" Two other friends, India and Marsha, had a similar problem. But even with Baba's written permission to stay, they had to account for at least six months they had spent illegally in the country without visas. Baba sat in his chair, grinning from ear to ear. In his hands was a white scroll. He already knew of their dilemma. Baba proceeded to read the letter. Gill squirmed - then interrupted, "*Baba, that's a lie! India and Marsha were not with you in Whitefield all that time.*"

The scroll in Baba's hand shuddered. "*Not a lie! Not a lie! Your mistake, your misunderstanding. God is everywhere. I am everywhere. Darjeeling, Whitefield, Prasanthi Nilayam is all with me. I wrote this letter out of pure love, divine love. Not a lie!*" The subject was closed. "*Faith is very important for sadhana for spiritual path,*" Baba said. "*Doubts are evil and enemies - doubts come from ego, envy, jealousy, hatred...all bad qualities.*"

In February, I returned to Whitefield with my fellow Baba devotees. Arriving late at night, we were dismayed to find that the 'Major's house' where we had stayed before was already occupied. Where could we go? I

16

had all but forgotten the two missionaries whom I had met a year previously, when they came to invite us all over for Christmas. Their offer, should we ever have need, now came to my mind. Arriving at the house, the door swung open and there was Mrs. Carroll, the missionary's wife, smiling warmly. Conversation wasn't light for long. Evidently the Carroll's had some kind of 'burden' for us, but I was no less zealous that the Carroll's should accept Baba, whose name, equally with Christ, meant Truth! There was a vital struggle between the two opposing systems of belief. Both could not be true at the same time.

The Carrolls pointed to one Christ and one occurrence of incarnation. *"Agreed"*, I said. Christ was a person in history as much as Tiberius or Xerxes. But he was also the Cosmic Christ, incarnated previously as an absolute principle. As such he has touched all scriptures in all forms. *"Where does it say that?"* the Carrolls asked. *"And how interesting that not once in the New Testament does Christ refer to any of the Eastern concepts of pantheism. If each man can pick and choose for himself what is true, where are you? If our basis for judgement is a private inner experience or intuition, well, experiences contradict. What standard could I use to discern the false from the true, the counterfeit prophet from the genuine article? For the Bible warns of counterfeit spokesmen for God, awesome in their subtlety of argument."*

The Carrolls defined truth in uncompromising terms. *"Man is at enmity with God,"* they said, *"separated from Him by a gulf of sin. The stupendous thing about God's grace to fallen and imperfect man is that he loved man in his sin. That love was shown in the space-time incarnation of the Logos as the long predicted Messiah, Jesus Christ."*

Now came the proclamation of utter exclusiveness that truly made Christianity the 'straight and narrow way'. Ivan Carroll opened his Bible.

"There is no salvation in anyone else at all," he read, *"for there is no other name, under heaven, granted to men, by, which we may receive salvation."* The narrow gate was to accept Jesus Christ exclusively as Lord and Saviour. Not bow down to any other - Buddha, Krishna, Chaitanya or even Sathya Sai Baba. I searched my mind for a reply. I told them of Baba's great love, and the goodness of the people surrounding

17

him. I gambled that such goodness would break through to the missionaries. But this introduced a whole new line of thought.

"A man can appear good and still be deceived. Our own seeming goodness is not enough to bring us into the full light of God. Scripture tells us 'none is righteous, no not one'. In fact there is no better salesman for counterfeit truth than a good man." This thought hadn't entered my universe.

Now Winona Carroll opened up her Bible. *"Satan himself masquerades as an angel of light,"* she read. *"It is therefore a simple thing for his agents to masquerade as agents of good."* My friend Surva Dass sought to stem the tide of this fanaticism. *"I just can't see someone running around with little horns and a tail."*

"The Bible doesn't ask you to believe Satan has little horns," the Carrolls replied. *"Think of the way Paul describes it: 'Our fight is not against human foes, but against cosmic powers, against authorities and potentates of this dark world, against the super-human forces of evil in the heavens'."*

The Carrolls attacked Surya Dass' idea that the Bible was directed mainly to highly spiritual initiates. On the contrary, Christ was reaching out to those whose only credentials were a humble, sincere hunger for God's love and forgiveness. Turning to his Bible again, Ivan Carroll quoted: *"Few of you are men of wisdom, by any human standard, few are powerful or highly born. Yet, to shame the wise, God has chosen what the world counts folly."*

I challenged the Carrolls to admit that they might not have total understanding of all the truths of scripture. They agreed, with commendable humility. But nothing shook them. By about 1:30 in the morning, it was finally time to turn in - but only after the most heartfelt prayer by the Carrolls that Christ would speak directly to our hearts and convict us all of the Truth through the Holy Spirit. We visitors nodded to ourselves knowingly.

I heard Surya Dass' footsteps near the front porch. I knew as soon as I saw his face that there was a surprise coming. He stood in the doorway, hands on hips, sighing and shaking his head slightly.

"Well..." he began and stopped. I guessed the rest of the sentence: *"...I'm not going to believe what you're about to tell me?"*

"Right!"

"It's about Sai Baba." My heart was beating furiously. *"Okay,"* I said, *"Let's hear the whole thing."*

"You know the teahouse in Whitefield? Well, I went in there and ran into some guys I've talked to a number of times. I got on to the subject of Baba. They wouldn't say a thing. Finally a guy called Raymond went for a walk with me near the Carroll's. He asked me to swear to keep this a secret. He said he had a sudden feeling of responsibility for my soul. So he was taking a chance, despite his fear of Baba's supernatural powers.

"Raymond told me that two years ago Patrick - the real good-looking Anglo-Indian with the long hair - went to the town of Brindavan one day and sat among a whole crew of Americans who were passing through. Baba thought Patrick was one of the freaks from the States. So he kept him for a private interview. When the others left and Baba got him alone, he did his usual number of materialising things and telling him his inner secrets, though I don't know why he didn't know that Patrick lived just down the road. Well, the next thing that happened was Baba reached down and unzipped Patrick's flies." I did not want to believe what I was hearing. The problem was, I knew it was true.

"Okay," I asked despondently, *"are you ready for this? Among the guys who Baba has 'purified' in the same way are Wendel, Phil, that disciple of yogi Bhajan, and 'Alpine' Schwartz. But that's not all...he has done it to me. But unlike Patrick, I did not respond. Up till now I've kept pretty quiet about the whole thing. I thought it was some form of tantric purification, or a test of allegiance."* We got up and started to make tea, wandering around in a daze.

"But there's another side of this," I added, *"there is an occult aspect about the semen. Phil told me that semen is used in really heavy occult stuff. The vital essence of life or whatever."*

We sat stunned, as the night passed, and continued talking into the early hours. Twenty-five years of being guided to this incredible peak, backed up by all kinds of complex life patterns, intuitions, omens and signs and an absolutely astounding philosophy. You invest all that you have and are in it, and in just a second, it's all ripped away.

Shedding quiet tears, wandering the fields around the cabin, I was never able to see beyond the dense cloud surrounding me. I had been tainted by something I did not fully understand. I cannot hope to convey this state of occult desolation, it has to be known to be understood. In grim loneliness, I struggled with the question, *"If I can be so totally blinded and deceived, then can I ever really know the truth after this? Will I ever be able to tell the true man of God from the false?"*

On my final day in Puttaparthi, I chose to go off alone up the hillside overlooking the *ashram*. I brought out my wrinkled *New English Bible*. Muddled and confused as I was, I still dared to search for the truth. Soon I was deep in it. Truly this book spoke as no other book - its searching honesty was unique, its stand on the way things were, utterly exclusive. I turned to Matthew 24, and a startling disclosure was revealed to me. I felt a fiery conviction as I read, *"Then if anyone says to you, 'Look, here is the Messiah', or 'there he is', do not believe it. Impostors will come claiming to be messiahs or prophets, and they will produce great signs and wonders to mislead even God's chosen, if such a thing were possible. See, I have forewarned you. If they tell you, 'He is there in the wilderness', do not go out; or if they say, 'He is there in the inner room', do not believe it. Like lightening from the East, flashing as far as the West, will be the coming of the Son of Man* [Jesus Christ].*"*

There was so much in this passage, I had to close the book and meditate. I filed it away as evidence for an alternative explanation of what Baba was. According to the Bible, he was one among many miracle-working deceivers. Then another fact began to sink into my mind. I had believed for all these years that Baba would reincarnate, assuming that he was the same part of Brahma as we all were. But that wasn't the meaning here in the New Testament. The long-promised Messiah entered the world by birth on only one occasion. Never again would he come through a human mother. This fact nullified the claims of every guru who claimed to be Christ come again. For when the ascended Son of man returns for the

20

second time it will be straight from heaven in power and glory. I went out into the starlight, broken and confused, to bring my despair before God, whoever and whatever He was. I uttered the Lord's prayer, at the end pleading with heavy heart to be shown by God Himself His true nature, without fear of deception. I prayed that God would open my eyes to the real truth, because I was unable to find it on my own. Behind locked doors in the Bangalore guesthouse, five of us held conference: Surya Dass, Mark, two other distraught ex-devotees and myself. I began to explain to the others why Surya Dass and I had left Baba. They were not altogether surprised - each had had inklings that there was an unwholesome sensuality beneath Baba's holy veneer.

They asked me who I thought Baba was. Shakily I repeated what I had read: *"Impostors will come claiming to be messiahs or prophets, and they will produce great signs and wonders to mislead even God's chosen, if such a thing were possible."*

"Then who is the real Christ?"

"Christ," I replied. It was so simple, so incredibly simple. I was beginning to see things in an entirely new light. It was dawning upon me in full power; I was not God. I was not even *a* god. I was Tal Brooke, a bleary eyed creature lost in the spiritual night. I told the others, *"This is what the Bible says we are. Creatures made by God. Mortal, vulnerable, flesh-and-blood people, made from the common elements, and God-breathed with a soul-life."*

I was ready now to concede that Christ is the only way, without need for any man, guru or celestial being. His is the most honest and simple salvation imaginable. It has to be that open, that honest, that straight, to be right for any man - not just a few chosen initiates who carve their own gateway. Some people have told me since, that when they were 'saved' or 'born again' nothing dramatic happened. But now, in front of the others, I was on trembling knees, praying with tears. I utterly renounced Baba. I admitted the depth of my wrongdoing. Repentance for me meant a heart repudiation of sin. I confessed that Christ alone is the way, the truth and the life. I bowed to Jesus Christ as Lord and asked Him to enter my heart, to take over the reins of my life. I got up a different creature - a man made new.

From Chaos to Cosmos

Discovering the true New Age

by
Alan Morrison
France.

It first began when I was very small. Thinking about God, the universe and all that. I must have been about eight when I said to my Mum on a bus: *"Why am I me and no one else?"* Looking at all the passengers I saw, in my simple childish way, that we each have our own space in the world, which every one of us is condemned to occupy for the whole of our lives. If I had a separate existence, with my own consciousness, then surely there must be a reason for it, a purpose to my life? *"Mummy, why am I me and no one else?"* No reply. That silence was an awesome chasm, which needed to be filled. Little did I know then that I would have to wait another twenty-seven years to discover the answer!

Never once in my entire life did I ever doubt the existence of God. In my childhood, God was a real person who was definitely 'out there'. Just from the forces of nature and the miracle of life, I knew there had to be a Creator. Even then, I also knew there had to be such a thing as Divine justice. When I became ill I used to wonder if it was because I'd been naughty and He was punishing me! I remember announcing to my parents when I was around ten years old that of all the religions of the world, only one could be right, or else they are all wrong. Even then, I knew that there were only these two possibilities.

I grew up in a Jewish home. We weren't in the least bit Orthodox. My father was a liberal, freemasonic Deist who said *"Next year in Jerusalem"* each Passover - but he had no intentions of going. I longed for something deeply spiritual all the days of my boyhood. I used to stand in the synagogue every Saturday waiting for it to happen. But I soon realised this was not the place for such things. One Sabbath morning, not long before my Bar Mitzvah (Jewish coming of age ceremony) I heard a man there praying over and over again: *"Please God, big boom"*. His prayer life was centred on the expansion of his business interests. He spoke for many. It was the beginning of the end of any hope for me in secular Judaism.

Three years later my world exploded. I was a passenger in a car which was being driven by an older friend. When he asked me to get something out of the glove compartment I discovered a book which was to take me on a pathway for the following two decades. It was a paperback copy of the *Tao te Ching* by Lao Tsu. This was what I thought I'd been searching for. It led me to a thousand and one other books which took me down a labyrinth of spiritual exploration. Inner space: that was the realm in which to travel. At last! I could get in touch with God - but He wasn't 'out there' anymore, He was somewhere within me!

Soon I became enthralled with the idea of spiritual evolution - that the human race is steadily advancing towards perfection here on earth, and that each one of us goes through an ever-improving series of lifetimes until that perfection is reached. I spent more than twenty years avidly devouring anything which I believed would get me further down that road. I became involved at various times with Taoism, Tibetan Buddhism, Theosophy, Anthroposophy, various Hindu gurus, Reichian therapy, Bioenergetics, Existentialism, the peace movement and many other fringe New Age activities. I was a classic product of the 'Swinging Sixties' - the 'sex, drugs and rock 'n roll' era, the 'ME' generation who were around twenty years old when Timothy Leary first said: *"Tune in, turn on and drop out."*

However, alongside all this spiritual investigation, two things kept coming home to me. The first was that somehow I never felt wholly involved in any of these activities. There was a sense in which I was always an outsider 'looking in'. It was as if there was some invisible barrier which prevented me from participating - as if I was being protected from an all-consuming involvement. This is something of which I was always aware from as far back as I can remember. The second thing that repeatedly came home to me was that, in spite of the benefits which were claimed for all the things I got into, the fact was that my life never really improved. In fact, it worsened - drastically - and somewhere in the midst of it all there was a heart of darkness which I could not yet identify. Looking back with the aid of hindsight I now realise that I deluded myself into believing that I was changing but, in truth, I was a sad, self-centred dilettante.

By the time I reached the thirty-fifth year of my life I was a burnt-out, ageing hippie with a massive record collection but no lasting relationships, plus an increasing disillusionment with everything I had ever been involved with. I felt as if there was nowhere left for me to run. Everywhere I looked I saw pretence and hypocrisy, especially in myself. I knew so much about magic, meditation, catharsis, liberation; but I couldn't break free from the prison of who I was, from the total emptiness within me. By now, I felt more in common with the existential 'outsider' than with the mystical time-traveller. This was the beginning of the end of the journey which had begun with the Tao of glove compartments.

Around this time I had begun to throw myself into self-destructive situations. Like Roquentin - the central character in Jean-Paul Sartre's 'La Nausée', a book which had became very influential on my thinking - I liked to live dangerously solely to promote an existential crisis. When a friend invited me to stay at one of the occult-inspired *Rudolf Steiner* residential schools deep in the heart of the countryside, I jumped at the chance to escape a world which was closing in on me. They soon asked me to leave, as they couldn't tolerate hopeless romantics who spend their time wandering the fields writing poetry and dreaming about a better world. But there was a particular night that I remember when I sat on the edge of my bed before getting in it. I looked down at my feet and saw myself as I had never done before. I remember feeling that I was at the very end of my tether. I suddenly realised that I had reached the end of the line in life. There was nowhere else to go, nothing else to be, unless something cataclysmic happened. I felt as if the next event in my life could only involve being plunged into a deserved vortex of death.

Suddenly, in the midst of all that despair, for some inexplicable reason, I prayed to Jesus Christ and asked Him to help me. I had never done anything like it before; neither had I heard of anyone else doing so. The only Christ I had ever known was the gnostic Christ who I believed to indwell all people unconditionally. Yet there I was, praying to the Man, Jesus Christ. I had only ever known Him from the few New Testament Bible passages I had read in the battered New English Testament which somehow had always been in my library. The Gospel of Mark chapter thirteen had always held a strange fascination for me. It portrayed Christ in bold colours. In those days, when I read the verses which described wars, earthquakes, famines and pestilences and which culminated in the words: *"These are the birth pangs of the new age"*, they meant something very different to how I now understand them. Later, after that makeshift prayer, I cried myself to sleep.

A few days afterwards, I visited a bookshop which specialised mainly in works on the occult and other related religious books. On the shelves I spied a book that I had never seen before. It was called *The Dark Night of the Soul* by John of the Cross, and was a work of Roman Catholic mysticism. I had always been interested in Eastern Mysticism but I had never before come across Christian Mysticism. I entered a strange new world of 'ladders of perfection' spattered with Bible quotations. I got my dusty old Bible off the shelf and began to read it.

Shortly after this I moved to live in a small community on an old farmhouse north of York, while trying to piece together the shattered fragments of my life. The Bible reading intensified and I began to experience a peculiar sensation. I felt as if I was being contacted by 'spirits from beyond'. At the time, this was the only way I could describe it - although I would come to understand it differently later on. Feeling rather spooked, I needed to get to the bottom of this. I remembered seeing an advertisement for the *Churches Fellowship for Spiritual and Psychical Studies* on a health-food shop notice board. I phoned up the local branch and asked them if they could recommend anyone I could speak to about the weird feelings I was having. They suggested consulting a spirit-medium to find out the identity of the mysterious force.

Shortly after this, I was walking down a street in London (attending a

New Age massage workshop) when I noticed a visiting card face down on the pavement. When I picked it up I saw that it contained the phone number of a well-known clairvoyant and medium. I now realised that something extraordinary was happening. I immediately telephoned the woman and said I wanted to make an appointment. She said she had been expecting me and that I was to come first thing the following morning. She also revealed that she had an important message for me.

That night I could hardly sleep. I felt as if I was being assailed on all sides spiritually. It seemed to me that I had become the battleground for contrasting forces of darkness and light. I knew that I was on the brink of some remarkable discovery and was filled with trepidation and awe. As I descended a staircase in the morning I felt an invisible force attempt to hurl me to the foot of the stairs. I had to cling to the banister all the way down. What on earth was happening? It was as if something was powerfully trying to prevent me from getting to this woman. But who or what? And for what reason?

The medium welcomed me at the door. She looked as if she hadn't slept for a month. She had sunken eyes circled with darkness. She spoke with a strange accent and wore black. When we sat down she proceeded to tell me many things about my life, going back to my early childhood, which were 100% true. Then she fell silent. She looked at me intently and said that she had just one thing to tell me which even she found puzzling and was not the kind of advice which she would normally give to her 'clients'. All she was getting through from her 'spirit guide' was that I should read the Bible. When I heard that I was amazed; because that was already what I was doing. In fact my reading of the Bible was going to be the crucial turning-point in my spiritual salvation.

From that point on, everything began to change rapidly. I embarked on a long period of intense Bible study which revealed to me that all the spiritual pathways that I had previously explored were nothing whatsoever to do with religious truth. I discovered a Christian bookshop and began to read Christian literature, the first item of which was *Matthew Henry's Commentary*. I knew no Christians at this point. All I had was my Bible and these new-found books. I soon realised that John of the Cross's book which I had found in the occult bookshop missed entirely the foundations of the Bible. It was as if I was being shown right at the outset that the whole sphere of Christian mysticism is a gross misrepresentation of Christianity which ignores the central truths of the Bible - namely, the Incarnation of the Son of God and His atonement on the Cross. (It had, however, under God's sovereignty, served its purpose in drawing me to the Bible, which I would otherwise have continued to ignore).

My big discovery at this point was that there is a mighty spiritual battle in this universe of which most human beings are wholly ignorant. I found that there had been a fall of angels near the beginning of the creation and that this had led to a fall of human beings. I soon realised that the 'Ascended Masters' and other discarnate entities (including the beings currently imposing as 'ETs' or 'aliens') which have been so influential in the development of the New Age Movement and the 'New Spirituality' are actually lying spirits, fallen angels whose main work is to deceive the human race into believing that they can rebuild a better world for themselves right here on this planet (the only truly 'Ascended Master' is the Son of God, the Lord Jesus Christ, who has ascended to heaven where he sits at the right hand of God the Father almighty).

God plainly showed me through the Bible that there is only one spiritual way of salvation. I saw that God Himself had come in the flesh as a human being into this world, in order to take the penalty for my sins as there was no way of me doing so myself. I set about praying to God to forgive me for all the foolish ways of my life, for having wandered so far from His truth, for having committed so many offences against His holiness. I couldn't repent enough! It was so wonderful to feel cleansed of all the occultism and other forms of darkness which had overtaken my life for so many years.

I then came to realise that my earlier feeling of being contacted by 'spirits from beyond' was nothing to do with 'spirits' contacting me; but that it was God Himself. I had simply perceived Divine communication in the only way I knew at the time. Filtered through my warped understanding, when God 'tapped me on the shoulder' (as it were), I read it as an occult experience. The Lord Jesus Christ said that no one can come to Him unless God the Father draws him (John 6:44). And draw me He did! He even neutralised that medium's evil 'spirit-guide' and instead induced her to tell me to read the Bible.

When I look back over all the elements of my long and often wayward search for God and His truth, I realise how the Lord Himself 'tailor-made' so much of my journey, in order that I should eventually be fully drawn to Him. All these things - the gradual disillusionment with the New Age, the Peace Movement and with Eastern Mysticism, the discovery of the book in the occult bookshop, my drawnness to the Bible, the strange feelings of spiritual communication, the discovery of the visiting card in the street, the consultation with the medium - these were really stepping-stones by which the Lord wooed me to Himself, as it were. This does not mean that He in any way condones all these elements. But just as He overrules the sin of human beings and orders them to be helpful to His own divine plan (e.g. the plot against Joseph by his brothers in the Book of Genesis, chapters 37-50), so He also demonstrates His control of the pre-conversion pathway of those He is pleased to draw to Himself.

I realised that an organization such as the *Churches Fellowship for Spiritual and Psychical Studies*, in linking the churches of Jesus Christ with the occult, is a gross affront to spiritual truth and the purity of God. My visit to the medium is certainly contrary to God's law, which forbids the consultation of witches, but God in His sovereignty and providence, can overrule even the most sinful of human events for His own special purposes. Especially this is necessary when ignorant unbelievers are being drawn to Him.

I realised then that God was not some force which is inside everyone unconditionally - some 'higher self' which can be kindled into action through inward-directed meditations - but that He was instead a personal Being who had a close concern and love for me personally. I realised that He is a God 'out there' with whom I can communicate and have a personal relationship. I also realised that the great problem of the human race is that we are all born into this world estranged from God, opposed by nature to His laws and in desperate need of being saved from this pitiful condition.

Around this time I remember driving in my car while listening to a Mozart choral work. It was a piece I had listened to many times and had enjoyed for many years - even before my interest in Christianity. I knew the words well; but that day they came to mean something to me that they had never done before. When I heard the choir solemnly intone the words: "*Agnus Dei, qui tollis peccata mundi, miserere nobis*" ("Lamb of God, who takes away the sin of the world, have mercy on us"), I was overwhelmed. I felt that this was the cry of my own heart - a cry which needed to be heard from the highest heaven. I was so awash with tears that I had to pull over to the side of the road. All I could say was: "*Oh Lord, it's all true. I know it. It's all true. You have taken the punishment for my sins. You have saved me.*" At that point, the words of Jesus, "*You must be born again*", became a living reality. I knew that I had been made anew. I had been both saved and assured of that salvation.

It was around that time that I found my way to a healthy church where I had fellowship with other Christians for the first time in my life and where I could learn more of the truths of the Bible and grow in grace. It was around that time that I met a young cellist who had recently been initiated as a Tibetan Buddhist, having spent some years exploring New Age avenues. But as she listened to me unfold the story of how I came to faith in Christ, she was drawn to explore the Bible for herself. It was not long before she too had renounced her Buddhism, having believed the Word of God and dedicated her life to the Lord Jesus Christ. Eighteen months later we were married in the Lord.

From that time onwards our lives have been dedicated to the God of our salvation and also to exposing the false spiritual pathways which ensnared us for so many years. I had finally been shown the answer to my childish question: "*Why am I me and nobody else?*" The reason: it is because each one of us has been made uniquely to glorify God and enjoy Him forever.

Meanwhile the world pitches headlong into ever-deeper confusion and rebellion against the one true God and the truth He reveals in the Bible. I firmly believe that the religious explosion which began in the 1960's involving hallucinogenic drugs, Eastern mysticism and self-exploration - and which has bewitched so many impressionable young people from that time to the present - was fabricated by the powers of darkness to bring that generation, and those ensuing, under their evil influence. The 'New Spirituality' - and the 'New World Order' which parallels it in the political sphere - is a dark work of the fallen angels being continually advanced as this rebellious world moves towards the climax of history.

For Jesus Christ, the Son of God, is going to return and bring things to a swift conclusion at the Day of Judgement, when all those who have renounced these works of darkness - confessing their need for salvation by a personal God who is 'out there' and coming to Him for forgiveness and new life - will become the population of the new universe which He will create out of the ashes of this present evil world. That will be the TRUE New Age!

It is my earnest prayer that all those reading this brief testimony will join me on this eternal journey, so that God, the Father, Son and Holy Spirit, will be glorified and shown to be the REAL Master(s) of the Universe.

Inside The New Age Nightmare

by
Randall N. Baer

Randall Baer's New Age involvement began in his teens when, like many of his peers in the 1960's and 1970's, disillusionment with the Church and traditionally patriotic ideals set in. By the age of 14 he was full of questions about God, the Bible and life, but sadly nobody was prepared to sit down and discuss things with him. In his own words:

"Something snapped in me. I no longer wanted to attend what I perceived as sterile and lifeless Church services and study groups. I suddenly knew that what I was searching for wasn't there. In the years ahead, I would hear many New Agers telling a similar story. I started going to various libraries searching for truth on my own. The realm of books, I felt, would open up the doors to new horizons."

Randall had a powerful urge to discover the truth about who he was, and who God was. He searched through books on religion, philosophy and the occult. At age 15, he began practising Hatha Yoga and meditation and had accepted the 'All is Oneness' philosophy of the New Age movement.

Although he was very successful at school and college, he turned to Marijuana in order to open up a 'deeper' spiritual worldview. He says: "One evening I felt that I had an encounter with what I thought was 'God'. While slowly inhaling the marijuana, all of a sudden the

31

surrounding room disappeared. I found myself floating in the cosmos beyond all sense of time. The boundaries of my body and sense of identity miraculously expanded as I became the 'light' and the 'light' became me. Feeling like I was effortlessly soaring through infinity, I believed that I had met 'god' and was one with the Universe. This was what the Eastern religious philosophies were talking about - pure oneness and enlightenment."

His world view rapidly changed and he began to see 'Nature' as the source of peace and truth. If he could really become one with it, like the American Indians, he would find answers to his questions. Wordsworth and Thoreau became two of his major inspirational writers. Randall recalls:

"Wordsworth wrote: 'Come forth into the light of things, let Nature be your teacher.' This became the driving theme of my search."

From Marijuana he progressed to LSD and hallucinogenic drugs.

"A succession of experiences with LSD, Mescaline, Peyote buttons, Psilocybin mushrooms, and hashish with others in my Asian Studies house 'blew my mind'. Catapulted into extraordinary dimensions beyond my wildest dreams, I rapturously explored what I felt were the indescribable 'heavens' of the supernatural realms. Incredible vistas of dazzling rainbow light, beings of pure energy, and mind expanding transformations unfolded with each new experience. I felt that the psychedelics afforded me access to the very essence of Nature and the cosmos. Here, I thought, I was privileged to know the innermost secrets of the universe known only to Mystics, Saints and Psychedelic voyagers.

"When I would read some of the books in the college courses I was taking on Hinduism, Taoism, Buddhism, Yoga and Western mystics, time after time my psychedelic experiences matched precisely with these traditions."

All was not well however, as Randall relates:

"A few years later, though, I had an LSD experience that should have warned me of the deceptions I had embraced. Shortly after gliding up a crescendo into the peak of the LSD 'high', an overwhelmingly powerful demon-spirit took possession of me. I was no longer in control of myself as this demonic force took over the reins. While part of me watched helplessly, the demon-sorcerer cast a number of powerful spells and gave me visions of hideous darkness. After several hours of tremendous inner torture on this 'bad trip', the demon 'blew my circuits' and left me like a rag doll. I could not speak for two entire days, and the psychological damage took six months to heal."

Randall rejected drugs as a shortcut to Nirvana and instead focused all his efforts on achieving enlightenment through 'natural' methods. He engaged in Buddhist chanting and Silva Mind Control. According to the writings of 'Seth', a famous spirit channelled through the trance-medium Jane Roberts, Randall's experiences were outlined and presented as 'higher psychic powers'. By doing Silva Mind Control, he hoped to train and develop his psychic ability and mind in the 'right' direction. During a course he experienced two spirit guides whom he describes as American Indians. He says with hindsight:

"What I didn't realise at the time was that everything in Silva Mind Control was based on occult philosophy. The occult was simply repackaged in a de-religionised, Western format that would be acceptable and even appealing to middle-class America. Inner counselling is a type of Biblically forbidden practice of 'acquiring familiar spirits', that is, inviting demons disguised as spirit-friends into one's life."

In his student days, Randall spent time in 'ashrams' in America, and became a disciple of the well-known Yogi, Swami Babaji. He also received a degree in Religious Studies after which he pursued a profession in holistic medicine. He became a naturopathic doctor after studying for two years and attaining a thorough knowledge of alternative medicine and New Age healing practices. He says:

"I went about opening up a 'Natural Health Centre' in a medium-sized city in East Texas. In a small, business-zoned house, I offered personalised health care programs, bodywork treatments, weekly 'Awakening Your Potential' classes, iridology analysis, meditation and Hatha yoga classes, health care products, and a host of other products and services. I even had a carefully planned 'deep relaxation environment' in one room where a special arrangement of colours, plants, aromas, art and subliminal tapes and New Age music was created to induce 'therapeutic deep relaxation'.

While running the 'Health Centre' he met Vicki, who was the director of a 'New Age Awareness Centre'. It was Vicki who introduced Randall to 'Crystal power' via her spirit guides. She gave him a 'power object' stone which had originally belonged to an American Indian medicine man. He describes his experiences with this quartz crystal:

"Only minutes after focusing on the crystal in a state of trance-like meditation, my consciousness was catapulted into electrifying domains of extra-natural light, the likes of which I had never before perceived. The upper part of my head felt like it wasn't there, like it had become invisible, as my awareness raced upwards at the speed of light. From a high distance, I could see in my mind's eye that my body was trembling and shaking as the power of the experience rattled through it. This was my 'crystal initiation' into an entirely different supernatural realm. Wow! Was this 'crystal power' or what?"

It was in the 1980's that Randall and Vicki were married and decided to move to Santa Fe, New Mexico because it was a 'Vortex area' - a place which attracts all sorts of psychic phenomena. Immediately they began to experience the paranormal. Randall writes:

"The spirit world began to speak to us explicitly and directly. All of a sudden Vicki would go into a trance. Then a spirit would come into her body and animatedly speak. I couldn't believe what was happening. The variety of spirits coming and going was astounding - I talked with spirits identifying themselves as 'Moses', 'Mozart', 'White Eagle', 'White Cloud', 'Serapis Bey', 'Ascended Master Kuthumi', 'Mary', 'Golden-Helmeted Ones', 'Green Ray Master' and a host of others. The power emanating from these spirits was overwhelming and entrancingly intoxicating."

These spirits told the Baers to call out in their meditations to the 'Space Brothers', who were part of the 'Intergalactic Space Federation' in the solar system. The extraterrestrials were coming together to assist Earth in its 'purification process' to take it to its evolutionary conclusion - the New Age. The spirits also said that the Space Brothers were working together with the 'Great White Brotherhead', a universal hierarchy of Ascended Masters, archangels, angels and other types of spirit beings who administrate and control all aspects of creation. Randall's task was to teach the techniques of Crystal Power so that many people would be 'activated into a higher consciousness of Light'. The 'Higher Councils of Universal Masters', the 'Supreme' spiritual beings had ordained it. Over the next few years the Baers set up a successful 'New Age Awareness Centre' in New Mexico, lecturing on and propagating almost all forms of New Age belief and practice. But Randall's real breakthrough came with the publishing of his books on Crystals and Sacred Science. These books were written under the inspiration of spirit guides. He says:

"Approximately three months after moving to the northern New Mexico area, my 'Spirit guides' gave me instructions to write a book on the subject of crystals... the spirit guides told me to take 12 quartz crystals and lay them out in a circle, to tape another one to the occult 'third eye' and to suspend a large pyramid overhead. I was to sit in the very centre of the crystals with my head underneath the pyramid. This was supposed to create a 'crystal energy field' having amplified 'higher vibrations' for receiving channelled thoughts from the spirit guides.

"To my amazement, as I would enter a kind of semi-conscious trance, discernible thoughts, inspirations, and pictures would appear in my mind. All this was not my own doing - the spirit guides were transmitting their thoughts and influences to me. My job, effectively, was to take notes and then shape up the material into book form."

Randall's book *Windows of Light: Quartz Crystals and Self-Transformation* (Harper & Row, 1984) launched him onto the American national circuit of New Age celebrities. This book was generally regarded as the best book on this subject in the world at that time. His second book, *The Crystal Connection: A Guidebook for Personal and Planetary Ascension* (1985) was marketed as an essential reference, 'light years beyond the rest'.

After a national tour Randall was acclaimed one of the top three

35

authorities on Crystal power in the world, alongside the famous Marcel Vogel. Health and business professionals, as well as famous celebrities, attended his 'Advanced Crystal Energetics Training Program'. Randall had by this time incorporated into his house what he called 'The Ascension Chamber', which also contributed to his national fame. It was a room filled with crystals, pyramids and occult symbols. He used New Age music, subliminal tapes and special trance-inducing equipment and films to encourage out of body experiences. But Randall's life was about to change dramatically.

"One night, while in the Ascension Chamber, my spirit was roaming some of the farthest reaches of 'heavenly light' that I had ever perceived. Waves of bliss radiated through my spirit...Suddenly, another force stepped in. What I saw was the face of devouring darkness! Behind the glittering outer facade of beauty lay a massively powerful, wildly churning face of absolute hatred and unspeakable abominations - the face of demons filled with the power of Satan."

He describes the ensuing conflict:

"My body was shaking involuntarily, sometimes rather violently. This nightmare continued without respite for a full week. I thought I was going stark raving mad. In a month's time, though, my grave situation gradually settled down to some semblance of sanity and normality."

Randall looks back and sees this experience as God intervening in his life:

"At this point, though, I only knew that some force greater than that of the devouring darkness had done two things: (1) It had shown me the real face of the New Age 'heavens' and 'angels' that I was so deeply involved with, and (2), it had delivered me from certain doom. What I knew at this time was that I had made some serious errors in my New Age involvement. I also knew that if those errors weren't corrected, I might face the same horrific experience again. And quite possibly the next time I wouldn't get away."

Randall turned to searching the Bible for answers. He compared scripture with New Age thought. The more he analysed it the more he discovered that the New Age picks and chooses what suits it from the Bible and discards the rest. He also discovered that he had broken God's laws and was separated from God by his sin, the consequences of which would be judgement and hell. As he read further he saw that God was so full of love that He sent His own Son, the Lord Jesus, to pay the penalty for sin (death) on the cross. There was hope - eternal life was available as a free gift. The God against whom he had sinned could forgive him.

Randall knew that he had become possessed by a demonic power and felt a spirit force taking more and more control until finally, the day came, when he repented of his sin and accepted Jesus Christ as his Lord and Saviour. He was watching a TV programme during which the gospel message was presented. At the end of the sermon, the preacher called on interested viewers to call on the name of the Lord for salvation and forgiveness. Conscious of his guilt and need of a Saviour Randall confesses:

"I was in such a state now that I was way past feeling self-conscious or silly...I gently dropped to the floor. As this happened I felt the conviction of the Holy Spirit pierce my heart and I wept in acute repentance... I had never prayed like this before...The Lord had cut through my horrific satanic bondage and set me free as he washed my scarlet sins as white as snow.

"With an absolute certainty, I knew that this was what I had been looking for all my life and never had found till now. This made even the most powerful mystical New Age experience completely pale in comparison... Satan's glowing counterfeit fineries are as cheap, filthy rags compared to the Truth."

Randall's conversion to Jesus Christ stirred up a storm of hostility. Some, like his wife Vicki, also renounced her New Age involvement and believed in the Lord Jesus Christ. Others became angry and abusive; especially when he began to expose what Randall now called 'the deception of the New Age Movement'. The little group of ex-New Agers suffered a good deal of persecution but through it all stood firm in their faith in the Lord Jesus.

Randall wrote a book, telling of his experiences and conversion to God called *Inside the New Age Nightmare* (Huntington House, 1989). The week it was published, Randall met with a puzzling and untimely death. Upon completing a lecture tour in New Mexico, during which he further exposed the New Age movement, his car ran off a mountain pass. Several investigations have been unable to uncover whether it was murder or an accident. One thing is sure, Randall is now in heaven in the presence of Christ, the Saviour he accepted when he turned from the occult and repented of his rebellion and pride. "For God so loved the world, that He gave His only begotten Son, that whosoever believes in Him, should not perish but have everlasting life" (John 3:16).

Outer Beauty, Inner Despair.

by
Caryl Matriciana
Hemet, California, U.S.A.

My father proudly opened the daily newspaper and saw my perky teenage face filling the page. At 18 I had launched into a modelling career! In time, success led me to feature on billboards, TV commercials and fashion pages in India, England, France and the United States. I rubbed shoulders with the 'beautiful people' of fashion and film.

On March 15th 1947, I was the last British baby born in Calcutta before India's independence. I arrived with a silver spoon in my mouth, surrounded on every hand by finery and elegance. My great-great-grandfather was the governor-general of Bombay. His children and grandchildren all played their part in the colonial life of the fabulous country of India in the days of the Raj.

My earliest memories are of the nuns in the Catholic School I attended and the summer trips to Darjeeling to escape the heat, from where we could sometimes see Mount Everest. Attending a boarding School in Madras brought me face to face with some of the unforgettable sights of India. Its people are etched on my memory forever - the beggars, the servants, the children, the holy gurus and the Maharajas.

As a child I had begun to discern the darker side of India's culture. Driving home from the Roman Catholic Church my sister and I could see icons and phallic stones on nearly every street corner. Barren Indian women kiss these stones in the hope of producing a male child. Many trees had altars at their bases. My mind was full of questions as I saw worshippers giving homage to such objects as cows and trees. There were pictures of deities in every little shop and market stall; Shiva, Vishnu, Kali and Durga. These terrifying gods frightened me with their intertwined snakes, protruding tongues and skull adorned necks.

I considered my Roman Catholic Church to be far superior to this 'pagan' religion of Hinduism. What kind of religion was it where cows were treated like deity and women were treated like property? The caste system appalled me. The depravity of urine drinking, dung bespattered Yogis or 'holy men', combined with the madness and chaos of the many Hindu religious festivals, made me thankful for small mercies.

After a spell at another boarding School, this time in England, I returned to India at the age of 17. However, two years later, political unrest and an increase in violence forced our family to move permanently to England, where I landed a job in an art studio in London and moved into a flat with my best friend Maggie. A job with the BBC working on TV projects kept the money coming in. I mixed with upwardly mobile young men and developed a socially arrogant attitude which was uncannily like the caste system I had so abhorred in India. Nightclubs, galas, theatre and film premiers, operas, horse races; it was life in the fast lane and I enjoyed it.

Greedy for more excitement and experience I handed in my notice and set off to travel round Europe with a friend. My live-for-today philosophy soon emptied my bank accounts and I returned to London to become a freelance artist. Success in modelling and film projects meant I could afford an apartment on the famous 'Kings Road' in Chelsea. I was proud to be one of London's swinging jet setters! Life was good to me - yet I recall the frequent feelings I had of deep, inner pain. I remember days of depression. I can still feel the loneliness and the struggle. I had everything, yet I seemed to be emotionally bankrupt. I was a slave of tobacco, alcohol, partying and promiscuity.

On impulse I married my business partner, Paul, but within weeks we angrily separated. I stared failure in the face. The girl who could do anything now had a business and marriage failure behind her. The experience was totally draining. I packed my bags and escaped to the Bahamas.

I worked on the Island Development Project, designing holiday homes for foreign clients. Through some of these clients I began taking hashish and marijuana until it was a daily habit. Days merged into weeks and months. The Island Development Project ended and I moved on to Miami in Florida to do further modelling and artwork. My drug use continued apace. In fact, my cravings had me rolling my first joint before getting out of bed in the morning. I became a fan of rock music and eventually took up yoga to gain 'more vigour, calm, strength, a higher IQ and sexual prowess'.

Every morning found me sitting cross-legged in my living room with eyes closed, arms relaxed and palms in my lap facing upward. Touching my third finger to my thumb added greater energy to the experience. I practised controlled rhythmic breathing, in through my mouth and out through my nose. I focused my imagination on an illusory object somewhere before me. What began as a physical exercise soon developed into a spiritual and mystical experience. I embraced Hindu philosophy. I sought to raise the psychic energy that I was told lay dormant at the base of my spine, to unite with the 'divine essence' or 'cosmic consciousness'. So deeply did I progress with yoga that I experienced the same thrills through meditation that I had attained through drugs.

In time, out of the body experiences and altered states of consciousness began to take their toll. Inner turmoil began to depress me in such a way that no therapy or psychoanalysis could touch it. I tried to control others by mastering psychokinesis and ESP. Yet true satisfaction continued to be an illusive, intangible dream. Relationships, jobs, money, travel, experimentation of various drug concoctions and thrilling mystical experiences - nothing satisfied my inner longings for peace and rest. Perhaps the Hindus were really right after all; reality is just 'maya', and illusion.

I reasoned out many philosophies with my new avant-garde friends. I bought into re-incarnation, transmigration of souls and other myths from

India. I became deeply involved in vegetarianism which, I convinced myself, was the purest form of self-cleansing and gratification. Somehow, not eating animals led to animal rights activism and, the healthcare aspects of vegetarianism blended themselves with Eastern spirituality and neo-pagan philosophical ideas (similarly, health aspects of yoga led me into an Eastern worldview too). I now believed animals were reincarnated souls, the earth - our mother and nature to be esteemed, respected and harnesses for its natural powers. Once I despised those who viewed the cow as sacred - now all animals had taken on a sacredness that superseded the worth of human beings.

My spiritual search went on for months. By now I had accepted the twin ideas that all paths led to the same God and that all beliefs were equal. I started to dabble in the concepts of the Hare Krishna movement, enjoying their food, music and culture in the Coconut Grove Community Park near my home. I spent hours reading their literature and learned the power behind their 'Hare Krishna, Hare Rama' hypnotic mantra representing all the sounds of the creative force of the universe. The endless chanting of this mantra is supposed to bring the devotee into mystical contact with his deity. The discipline and purpose of the Krishna's gave me a new goal in life and made me desperate to 'belong'. George Harrison of the Beatles was my hero, and he was actively promoting His Divine Grace Bhaktivedanta Swami Prabhupada, the founder of the Krishna movement, as the 'true guru'. My experience of the Krishna movement ended in bitterness as I saw them only interested in converting the rich and famous in order to acquire their money. Despite my eagerness to convert, I was ignored and rejected. As I look back I thank God for the way things worked out.

While on a TV commercial shoot in Florida for a European martini, I became enchanted with one of the leading male models called Denny. Our fairytale romance was a passionate love story suddenly and cruelly, as fate would have it, curtailed because my United States visa ran up against complications. I was given 24 hours notice to return to England where I fought bureaucracy and lost. In desperation, we reunited later in Canada where dramatically Denny then smuggled me over the U.S. border. Instead of the pressure drawing us together, it only aggravated our emotionally packed relationship which rapidly deteriorated. One bitter cold morning, after yet another row, my hopelessness sent me roaming the Chicago streets until I came across a large Roman Catholic Church. I entered the sanctuary making the sign of the cross across my broken heart. The surroundings were welcoming and familiar. I knelt at the altar and in desperation prayed, *"Oh God, please help me."* I stayed there for a long time gazing at Christ hanging on the cross. I was touched deeply at the thought of the hurt and mutilation that He had suffered in His death.

Some days later, I accompanied Denny on a modelling job. Models and crew gathered in a cheerful green park near Lake Michigan to shoot for a *Sears Roebuck* catalogue. During a break I eavesdropped on a conversation between two men on the shoot. *"Jesus Christ is the only way to God,"* I overheard Charles say to John. *"What an outrageously intolerant statement that is! "* I heard myself snap back to Charles, before I even realised I had rudely butted into the conversation. *"All paths lead to God,"* I continued, *"How can you make God so small that He can only communicate through one path? What about all the African and Red Indian tribes in the jungle that don't even know about the Jesus path?"*

I dismissed Charles' attempts to answer my points because he insisted on quoting the Bible as the only authority. This was so arrogant, I thought - what about all the other great books and teachers? I felt I'd won the argument with Charles because he seemed at a loss for words and I'd got the last ones in anyway! Little did I know, from that day on, Charles began to pray that God would break my hard veneer and reveal Himself and His Son, Jesus Christ, to me.

A few days later John asked Denny and me to come and meet some of his new friends. Unknown to us, John had now become a Christian. After a good deal of persuasion we agreed to go, but we insisted *"we can't stay long."* John took us to Old Town, Chicago. On the way we passed by some 'amusing sights' on the streets outside. Transvestites in outrageous garb, prostitutes touting for business, pornographic shops flashing neon signs advertising various outrageous films and gimmicks. We giggled at it all. We detoured along Madison Avenue admiring all the fashion shops. The nightlife of Chicago excited us, until we reached the Old Town section, where we were in the heart of the 'arts and crafts' scene. The informal 'get-together' we were going to was held in the back of a brightly-lit bookshop. We walked through the shop and arrived in a cosy back room. Everyone glanced up and smiled at us warmly. As they moved over to make room for us I thought, *"What a friendly bunch of people!"* As I glanced at their joyful faces I wondered what kind of dope they were on, but I couldn't smell the familiar marijuana smell.

Everyone's attention turned to Richard, a skinny looking chap with a gentle Canadian accent, who stood up and began speaking to the group. At first I took no notice of his speech. I was fascinated by the people around me. They seemed so natural and unaffected, quite unlike any group of people I had ever been with before. As my eyes moved towards Richard again, I tried to focus on what he was saying. He was speaking with strong authority and conviction. He picked up a well-worn book from beside him and started reading from it. It was really interesting. I wondered what it was. As the talk progressed it dawned on me that the book was a Bible! All of this was shocking to me. Outside of my schooldays' religious education classes, I had never been exposed to a group of contemporaries discussing the Bible. It was clear that Richard, the speaker, spoke as if he knew God personally, as a friend. Here I was, still wondering if God was a personal entity at all.

Before I knew it, an hour-and-a-half had passed. The message I had heard had introduced me to a concept of God quite different to that I received either in Roman Catholicism or in the New Age movement. After Richard closed his talk, there was a spontaneous time of prayer. The group was all absorbed in deep communion with closed eyes. As they spoke reverently to God on a one-to-one basis, I remembered the last religious discussion I had with a group of people - the Hare Krishnas. The Krishnas coldness contrasted with the warmth and genuineness of John's friends.

After the 'meeting' was over, I gravitated to Richard and thanked him for his words. He asked me a strange question: *"How long have you known Jesus Christ as your personal Saviour?"* *"I have been a Roman Catholic all my life,"* I answered. He tried again with a change of wording: *"When did you accept Jesus Christ as your Lord?"* *"Er, well, I don't know!"* I replied, a little puzzled. Richard was very patient with me. He gently probed further, *"Well, do you believe that Jesus Christ is the Son of God and that He died for your sins on the cross?"*

I considered this question deeply. I remembered vividly the cross I had gazed on for hours just a few weeks ago. While deep in thought Richard continued, *"Do you know that God loves you so much that while you were unaware of Him, and while you were still a sinner, He sent His own Son, down from heaven, to save you and to bring you into a relationship with Him? The word [Jesus] became flesh! Do you know your sins separate you from God, today and for all eternity, but through accepting the love of Christ you can be in the presence of God forever."*

I hung on his every word, yet this last statement drew a frown from me. My New Age background made me think I had been in the 'presence of God' all my life. Also, in New Ageism, or neo-paganism, there is no concept of being a sinner, or that our supposed sinfulness can separate us from being a god type: there is no sense of the possibility of separation from god-consciousness for a reincarnated eternity either. Richard explained further, *"God's character is only made up of goodness. He can't unite with anything bad. Jesus is equal with God because He is God's word and therefore sinless - perfect. He is the only remedy able to cleanse you from your imperfection. You wouldn't use dirty water to wash yourself clean would you? In other words, you can't clean yourself through your own means, you need God's way [His Son] to purify you."*

I was shocked by the simplicity of God's plan. Was I to do nothing to save myself, except to repent and accept Jesus Christ's work, and Him as my Lord and Saviour? I remembered the many times I had completed the 'Stations of the Cross' around various Roman Catholic Churches and the hundreds of masses I had attended. Did this not count with God? What about the Rosary and all the other religious rituals I had performed? Had all my religious efforts been futile?

I stared at my feet in the heavy silence. At last I looked up. *"Do you mean that what Jesus did on the cross is completely sufficient and that He is all I need?"* Richard nodded gently. Suddenly it became clear to my mind with full force. I had spent my life in one long futile effort to cleanse myself with my own dirty water! The dark knot of pride in my soul was beginning to untie.

"But what about all the wonderful spiritual experiences I have had in yoga and drugs?" I asked. *"It's all a counterfeit"* Richard said. *"I*

know, I've been where you are. These things are from lying and betraying spirits who mean to deceive you. It is Satan's job to give you whatever pleasure you want as long as it keeps you from the truth."

Neither Denny nor I had ever heard explanations like this from the Bible. Richard urged us to admit we were sinners, to turn from our sin and thank the Lord Jesus for dying in our place on the cross. He quoted a Bible verse which says, that if you confess with your mouth that Jesus is Lord and believe in your heart that God has raised Him from the dead, you will be saved (Romans 10:9). My eyes lowered. Tears fell to the ground as I was overcome by a sense of shame before God. I remember praying, gently confessing that I was a wretched sinner. I believed that Christ died in my place on the cross - for my sins. I was overwhelmed by His unwarranted love for me through this act. There were no bright lights or tingling sensations, only deep remorse mingled with gratefulness, a sense of peace in reconciliation and assurance of security for eternity. I had confidence in Christ and a joy and safety I'd never known before. As we drove home, the scenes that had amused me earlier took on a different significance. Suddenly I felt a deep sadness. What had attracted and fascinated me only hours before now appeared so empty. God was changing me! I saw how lost I'd been and how deluded the world was about Jesus Christ.

God's miraculous hand worked swiftly in my life. He released me from my longing for nicotine. I had been on 50 cigarettes a day, now I didn't crave one. My habitual addiction to drugs and dependency on alcohol were taken away too. On Richard's recommendation I read from the Bible - the book of Romans first. The Word of God was washing me, clearing my head, changing my thoughts and redirecting my spirit. It was amazing! Gently, God taught me new values. One was that Denny and I were in an adulterous relationship. I was flabbergasted! I knew I had to return to the husband I'd left behind in England and give up the man I loved in the USA. I was illegally in the USA too and that had to be rectified. Six weeks later, with bittersweet resolutions I left behind everything I'd cherished in the USA to embark on a new adventure. My self-centred life was being redirected. With a grateful soul and a new-found strength, I began anew. I'd found the greatest treasure of all, the gift of reconciliation with God through Jesus Christ, His Son.

TO THE READER

It may be that you, as a sincere seeker of truth, have identified with some of the experiences found in this booklet. In the course of your search perhaps you've tried some or all of the paths and beliefs in the true-life stories in this book. The fact of the matter is that yoga, religion, the higher self, channelling, psychology, reincarnation, self-realisation and healing therapies will not bring you closer to God or the truth. There is something in your life actively preventing such a breakthrough. It is absolutely vital that you understand this. Back in the beginning a perfect relationship existed between man and God. The world that God created was a perfect Paradise and Adam and Eve were sinless beings.

GOD   PEOPLE

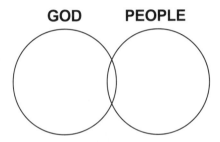

However, our first parents rebelled, broke the only law God gave them, and went their own way. The human race they fathered has lived in a state of alienation from God ever since. Like Adam and Eve you have also broken God's laws and therefore, in the words of the Bible: "*Your iniquities* [wrongdoings] *have separated between you and your God*" (Isaiah 59:2).

GOD   PEOPLE

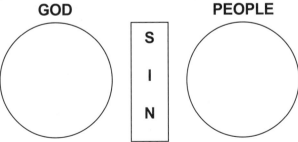

God's law says, '*Thou shalt not take the name of the Lord Thy God in vain*'. Have you ever said 'Jesus' or 'Christ' as a substitute for a four-letter swear word? Then you've broken this commandment. God's law also says, *'Thou shalt not commit adultery'*. Have you ever done that? The Bible says in another place that just looking at a woman lustfully is committing adultery in your heart! Who can claim to be free of guilt on this score?

God's law says, *'Thou shalt not steal'*. Have you ever done that? If you've stolen something, no matter how small its value was, what does that make you? Yes, that's right, a thief! God's law says, *'Thou shalt not bear false witness'*. To 'bear false witness' means to tell lies. Have you ever done that? Why, of course, you say, everyone has. What does that make you? A liar!

Furthermore, the Bible says that on judgement day God is going to *'judge the secrets of men'* (Romans 2:16). Think about that. Not only will you face the music for breaking God's laws; He is also going public with all your secrets. When this happens, do you think you will be declared innocent or guilty by the judge of the universe?

If you have faced this examination honestly, your conscience has already agreed with God and owned its guilt. You stand condemned by your own thoughts, words and deeds. Now ask yourself this question; what will my destiny be for eternity, heaven or hell?

At this point, many people, having realised they have broken God's laws and are facing judgement, start trying to merit God's favour by all sorts of good works and religious activity. Perhaps you've already tried this. The reason you have been frustrated and unsuccessful is because the root problem of your sin is still outstanding. Perhaps you've lived all this time, hoping that on judgement day God will balance your good deeds against your bad deeds and let you into heaven. Or perhaps you think He is so good and loving, He'll just let you off and sweep it all under the carpet. But, think about it this way. A man is in Court for serious fraud. As the judge is about to sentence him, the guilty man says, *"Hey, wait! You've forgotten about all the good things I did and how religious I was. And besides, you are too good and loving to condemn me."* Do you see the point? A crime is a crime. It has to be paid for; so the judge fines the man £50,000. The law demands it.

In the same way, God's law demands the death penalty on your law breaking (sin). God's prison for guilty sinners is hell. And it goes on forever. If you are thinking *"I'll take my chance, hell can't be that bad"*, you need to read Luke 16:19-31 in the New Testament. Hell is a place you want to avoid at all costs. The situation looks hopeless doesn't it? You're basically doomed. Perhaps you're thinking, *"How can I get round this dilemma?"* The truth is you can't. You can't play games with God. He won't compromise with your sin. You must pay the fine. Think about that for a while.

But wait! Let's go back to the courtroom. Imagine a rich man comes into that scene and, seeing the criminal condemned and guilty and repentant about for his sins, offers to pay the £50,000 fine for him. That would free the criminal from the demands of the law wouldn't it? He would be a free man: providing he was willing to accept the payment, of course.

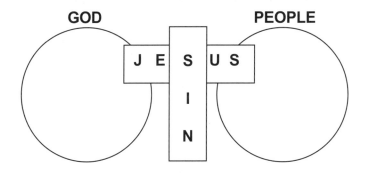

In Romans 5:6 the Bible says *"Christ died for the ungodly."* Who died? Christ. Had he broken any of the 10 Commandments? No. Did he have any secret sins? No. Why then, did He die? Read the verse again. Are you ungodly? Yes, we've already established that. Read the verse again. Do you see anything?

Now read verse 8: *"But God commends His love toward us in that while we were yet sinners, Christ died for us"*. Do you see what the Bible is saying? God loved you so much that He sent His Son, the Lord Jesus, to pay your fine. When Jesus died on the cross he died in the place of guilty hell-deserving sinners. No one but Christ could have done that, because only He is the sinless Son of God.

Let's draw this to a close by looking at one of the Bible's most famous verses, John 3:16. Read this verse slowly and carefully: *"For God so loved the world that He gave his only begotten Son* [Jesus] *that whoever* [that's you] *believes in Him should not perish* [go to hell] *but have everlasting life."*

What does it say you have to do to get everlasting life and be sure of not perishing? Just three words; believe in Him. That means this - if you have a proper sense of the dreadfulness of your sin against a holy and righteous God and you are willing to turn from that sin for ever, God wants you to know that His Son, the Lord Jesus Christ, died for guilty sinners on the cross, 2000 years ago. Are you a guilty sinner? What did Christ do on the cross for you? Can you not see how Christ's death on the cross meets the demands of God against your sin?

If you understand who Christ is and what He has done by dying and rising again, I urge you to repent and believe in Him at once. There's nothing more to do. One final verse may help you to see the simplicity of true salvation. John 3:36 says, *"He who believes on the Son* [Jesus] *has everlasting life: and he who believes not the Son shall not see life, but the wrath of God abides on him."* Can you see two halves to this verse? Which half are you in, the second half or the first? Do you have everlasting life? Are you saved? What are you depending on to get you to heaven?

Read the verse again. God is stating a promise to you today, just now where you are. You have no time to lose. Life is too uncertain. You only have *now* to make things right with God; to repent and trust Christ as your Lord and Saviour. Won't you turn and believe this very hour? He's your only hope. Don't trust religion or good works: trust Christ at once. Accept *His* payment for *your* sin. Since Christ has met the demands of God's law and paid its penalty, you can be free today.

If you have repented and trusted Christ as your Lord and Saviour:

After being saved, you should immediately take the following steps:

1) Thank Him for what He has done for you and ask yourself the question, *"What can I now do for Him."*

2) Start speaking daily to Him in prayer from your heart, bringing Him praise and thanksgiving, as well as asking Him for blessings.

3) Get a Bible and start reading and studying it. It's best to begin with the Gospels (e.g. Mark or John) and read through the New Testament. Ask God to give you understanding on how to apply it practically to your life.

4) Find a Bible believing Church and attend its meetings every week.

5) Tell others what the Lord has done for you.

If you would like confidential help or further information, please feel free to contact us. We can supply free Christian literature and addresses of Bible believing churches in your area. Our address is:

Penfold Books
P.O.Box 26, Bicester, Oxon, OX26 4GL, England.
Tel: + 44 (0) 1869 249574   Fax: + 44 (0) 1869 244033
E-mail: penfoldbooks@characterlink.net   Web: www.penfoldbooks.com

If this book has been a help to you please let us know.
We greatly value the feedback we receive from our readers.

ACKNOWLEDGEMENTS

The life stories in this booklet have been published with the kind permission of each individual featured. In Randall Baer's case, who is now dead, we are thankful to *Huntington House*, Lafayette, Louisiana, USA, for permission to print his story.

Also available in this series:

Angels of Light
5 Spiritualists Test The Spirits

Messiah
5 Jewish People Make The Greatest Discovery

Pilgrimage
5 Muslims Undertake The Ultimate Journey

They Thought They Were Saved
5 Born-Again Christians Recall a Startling Discovery

Witches & Wizards
5 Witches Find Eternal Wisdom

Light Seekers
5 Hindus Search For God

Copyright
Penfold Books © 1998

Published by:
Penfold Books
P.O. Box 26, Bicester, Oxon, OX26 4GL, England
Tel: + 44 (0) 1869 249574 Fax: + 44 (0) 1869 244033
Email: penfoldbooks@characterlink.net
Web: www.penfoldbooks.com and www.webtruth.org

ISBN: 1-900742-06-3